STANDING IN LINE:
COFFEE SHOP DRAWINGS

TM GIVENS

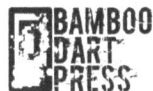

LOS ANGELES † NEW YORK † LONDON † MELBOURNE

Standing in Line: Coffee Shop Drawings by TM Givens

978-1-962316-01-9   Paperback

978-1-962316-02-6   eBook

Copyright © 2024 TM Givens. All rights reserved.

Cover art by TM Givens

Layout and design by Mark Givens

For information:

Bamboo Dart Press

chapbooks@bamboodartpress.com

Bamboo Dart Press 049

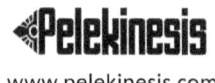
www.pelekinesis.com

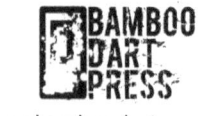
www.bamboodartpress.com

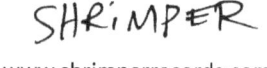
www.shrimperrecords.com

STANDING IN LINE:
COFFEE SHOP DRAWINGS

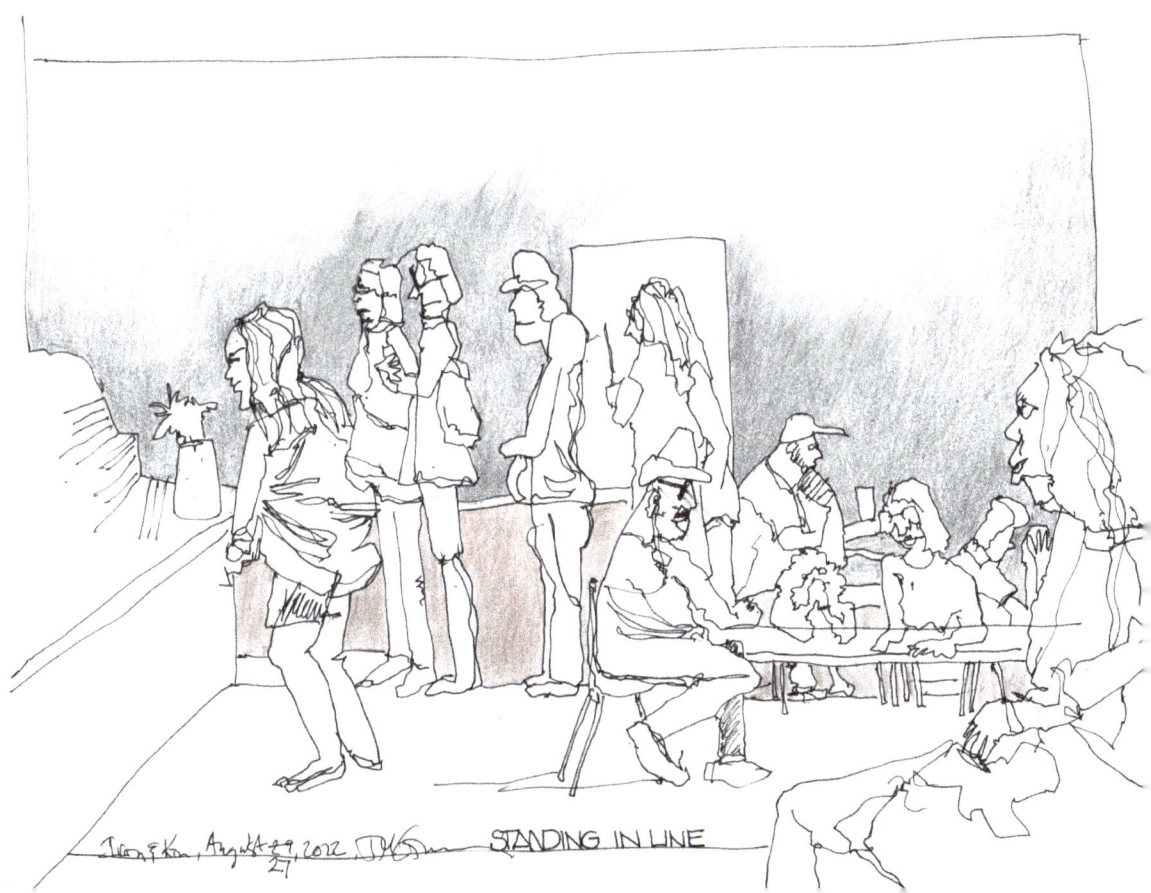

STANDING IN LINE

Sitting at the coffee place "Iron and Kin"
there was a variety of individuals

they gathered, talked, were alone
students
and each had an amazing wardrobe

sometimes the lines for service were
out the door and even the building
especially at Christmas with Santa Claus

most of the time people brought their little or big dogs
most on a leash

and even their children
babies in strollers,
toddlers to run and play,
teens to sit and gossip

and I made drawings of them…

old
young
faces were scrunched
clothes were multi - colored
arms were folded
hands in pockets
tall,
short
happy
sad
near
far way
and I was fascinated.

—TM Givens, June 2024

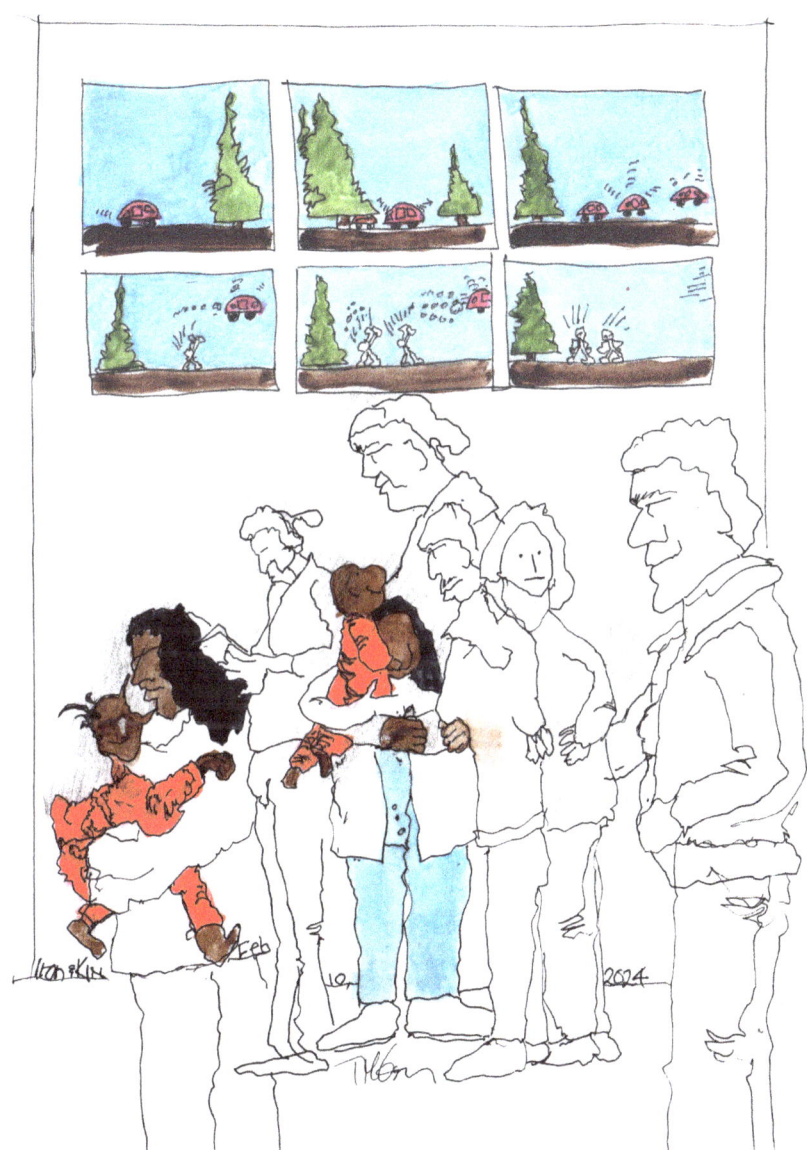

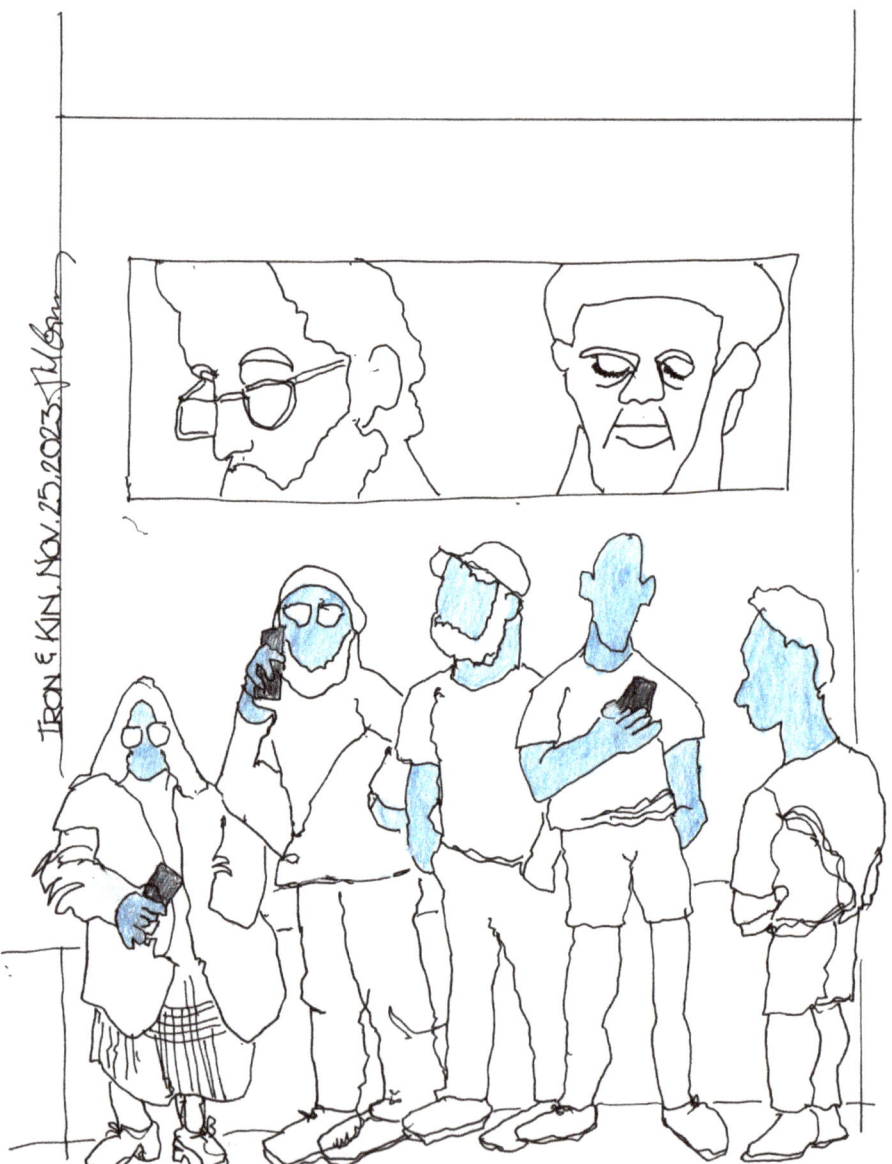

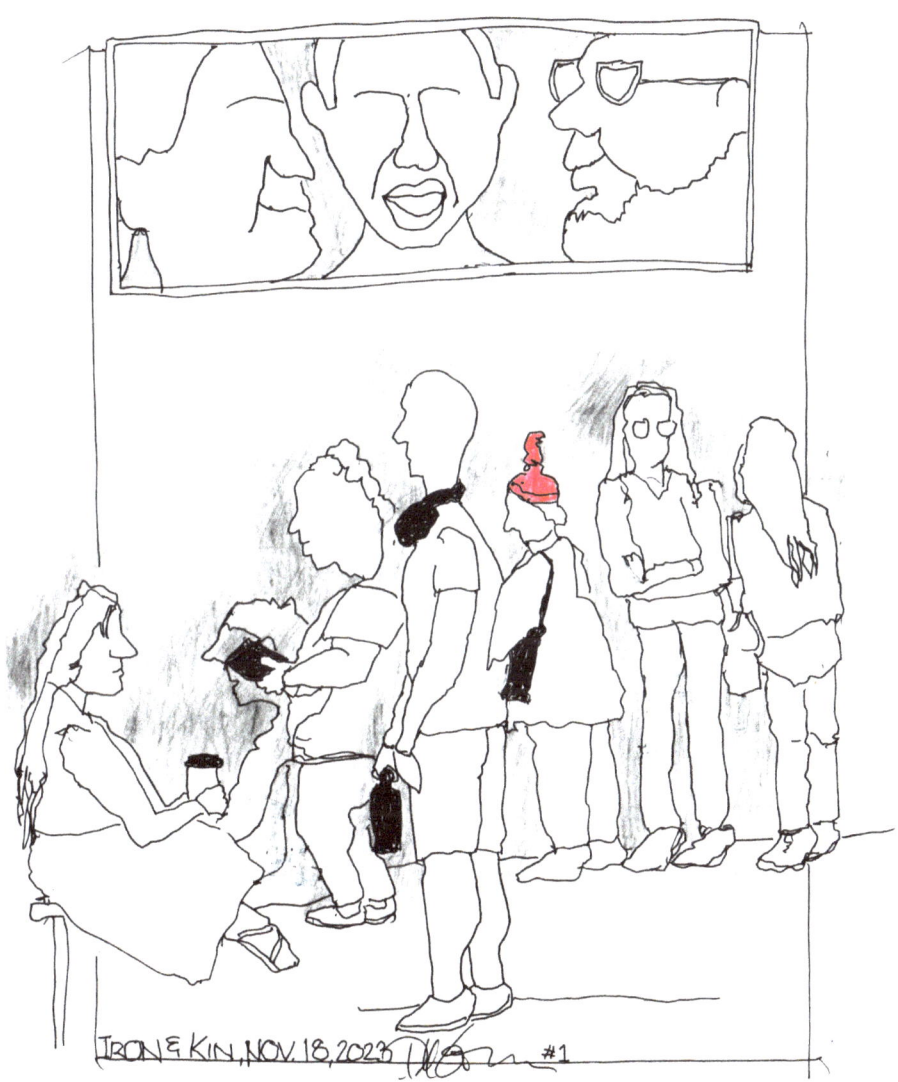

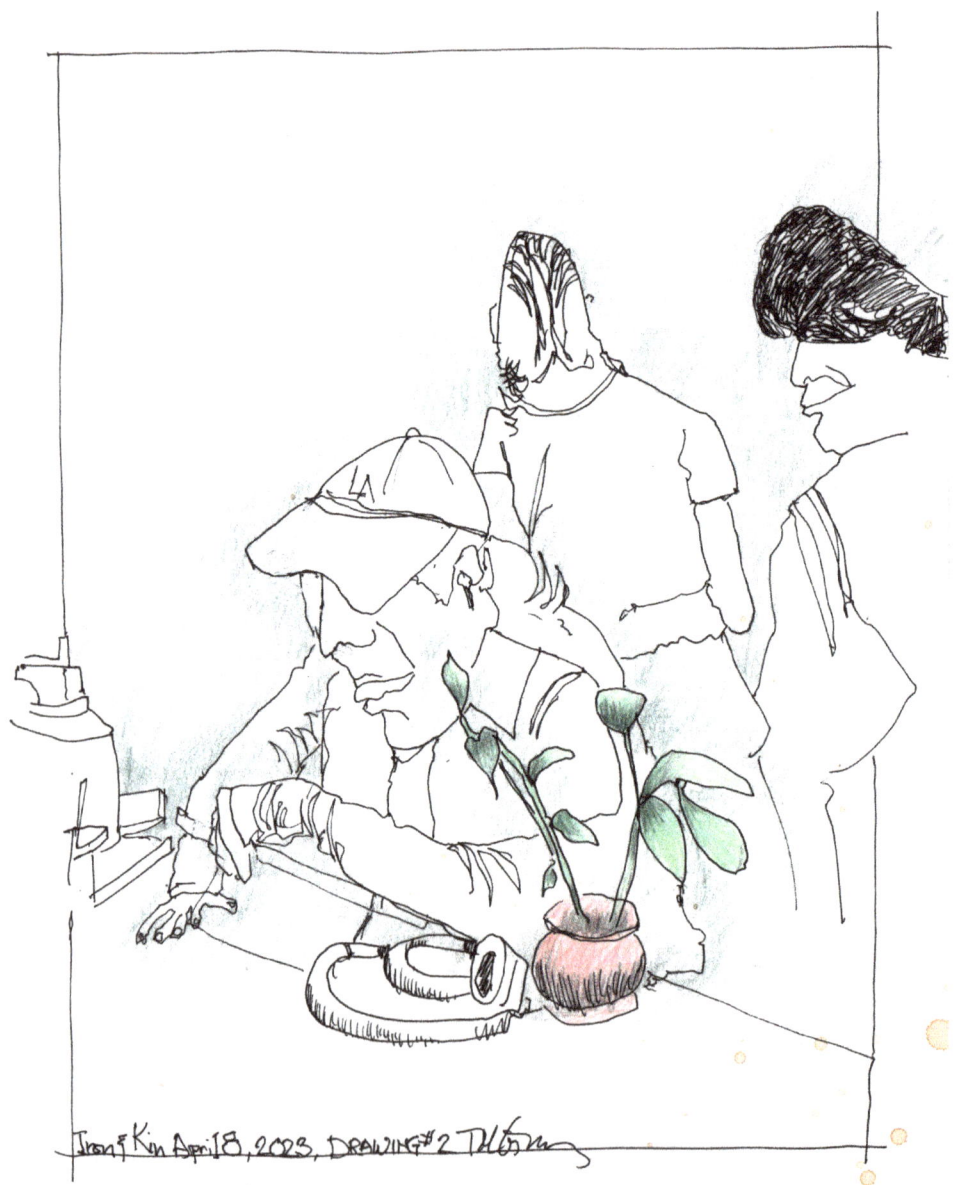

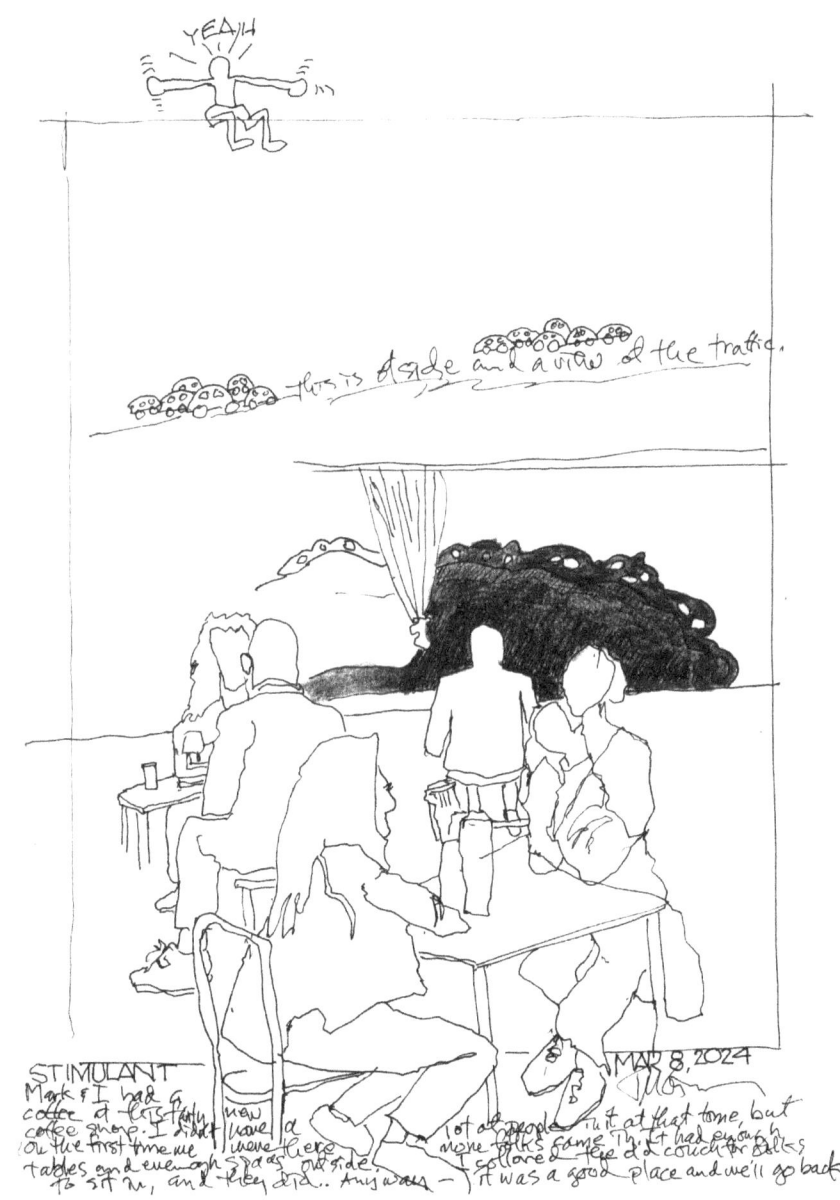

STIMULANT — MAR 8, 2024

Mark & I had a coffee at this fairly new coffee shop. I didn't have a lot of people in it at that time, but on the first time we were there more for this game. It had enough tables and enough space outside colored tile & a couch for Balk's to sit in, and they did... Anyways — It was a good place and we'll go back.

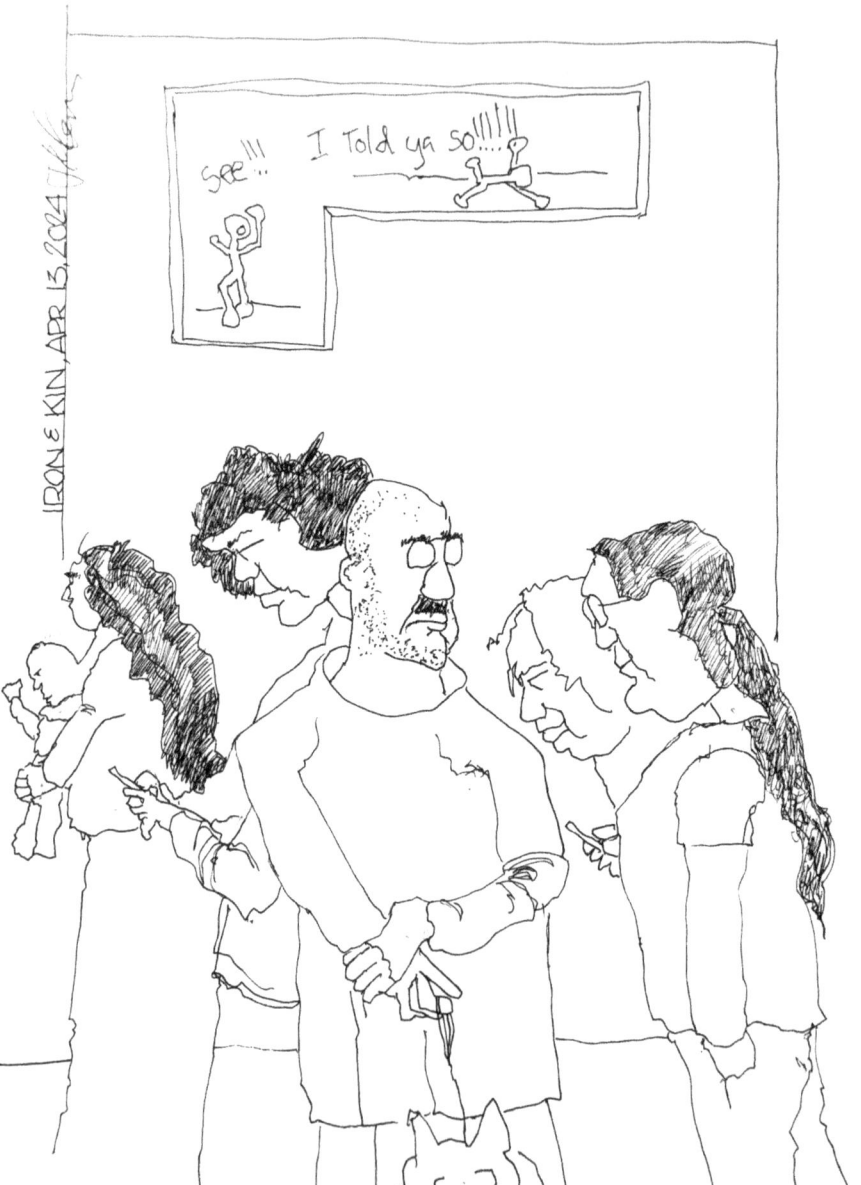

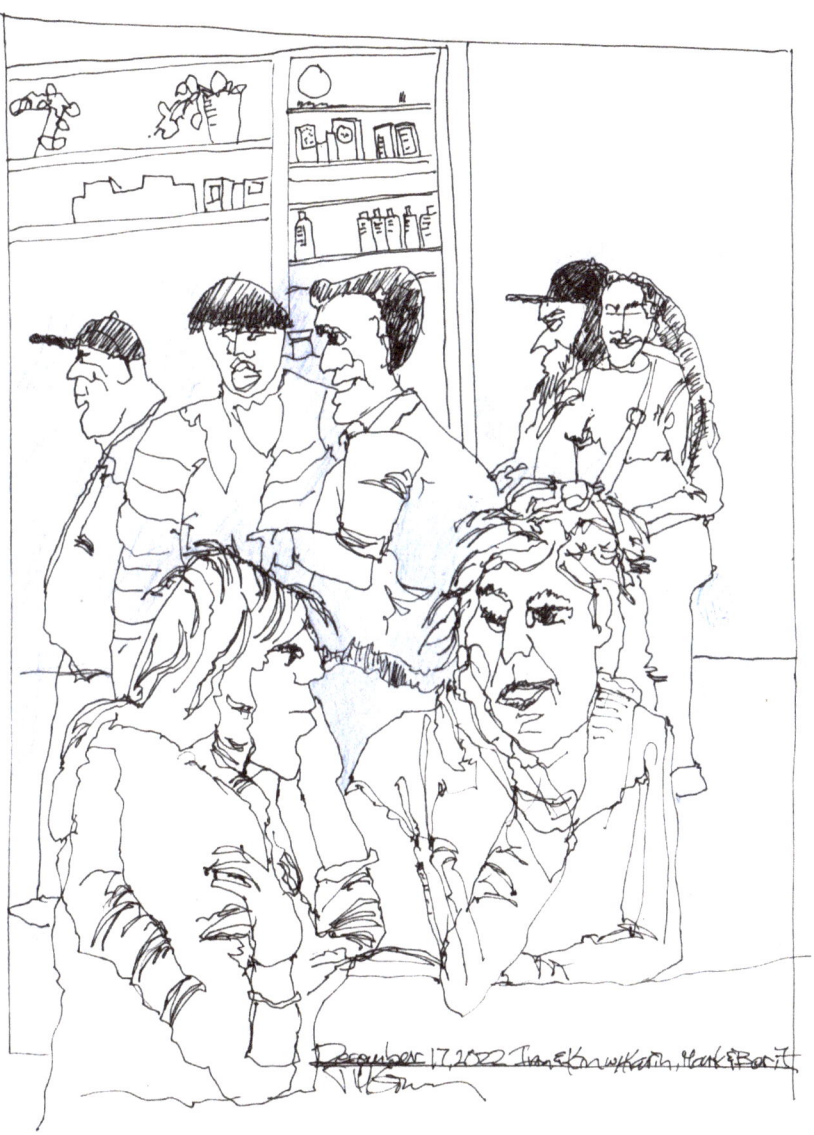

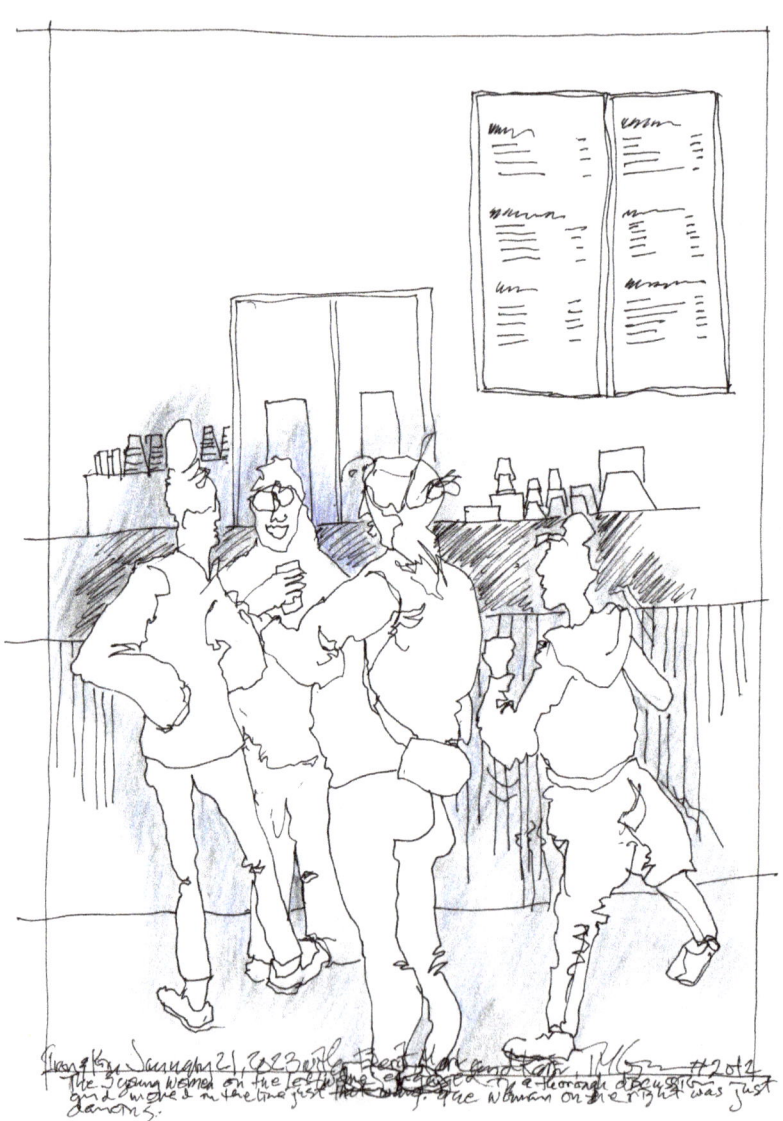

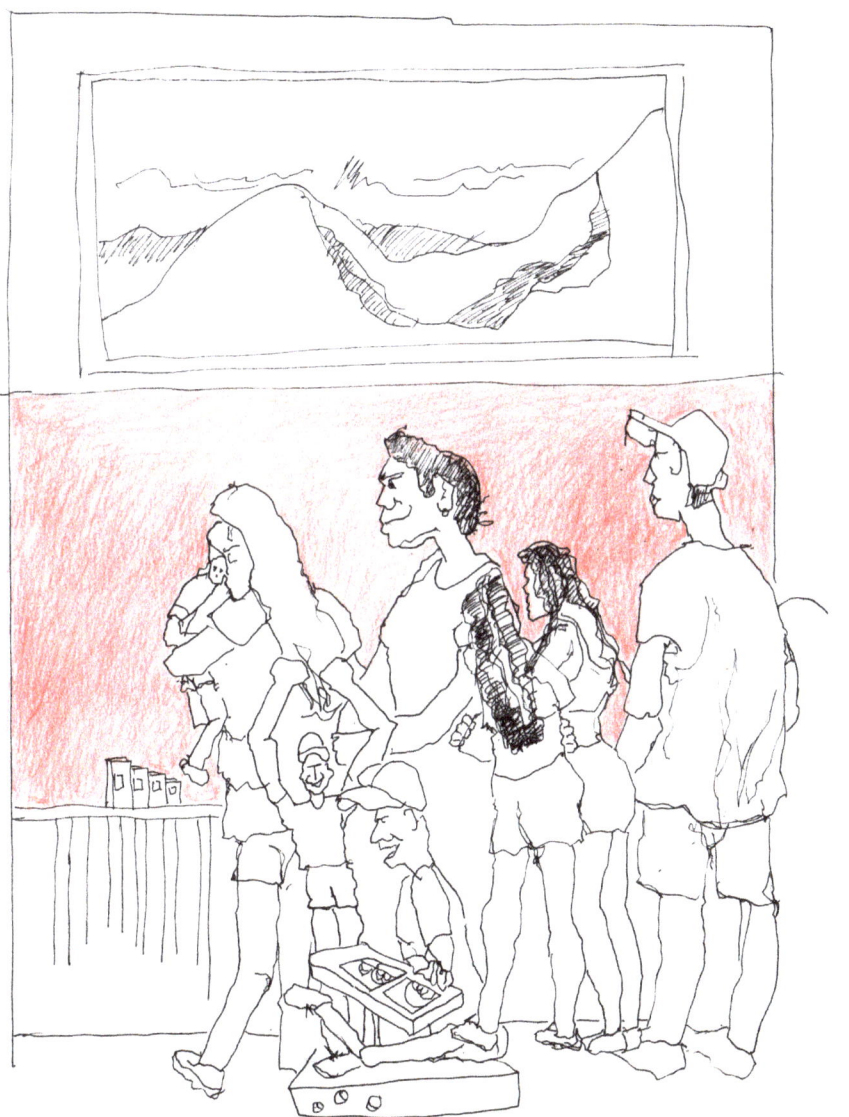

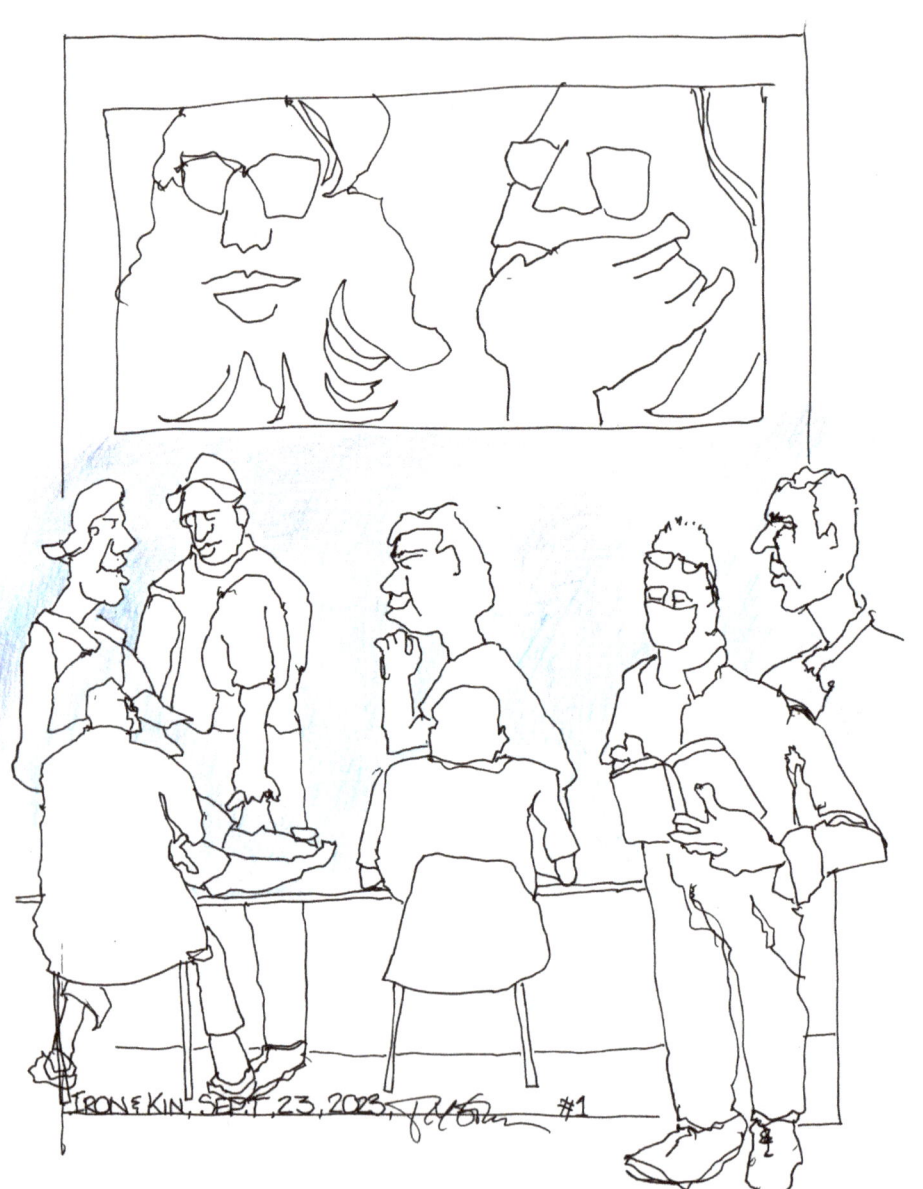

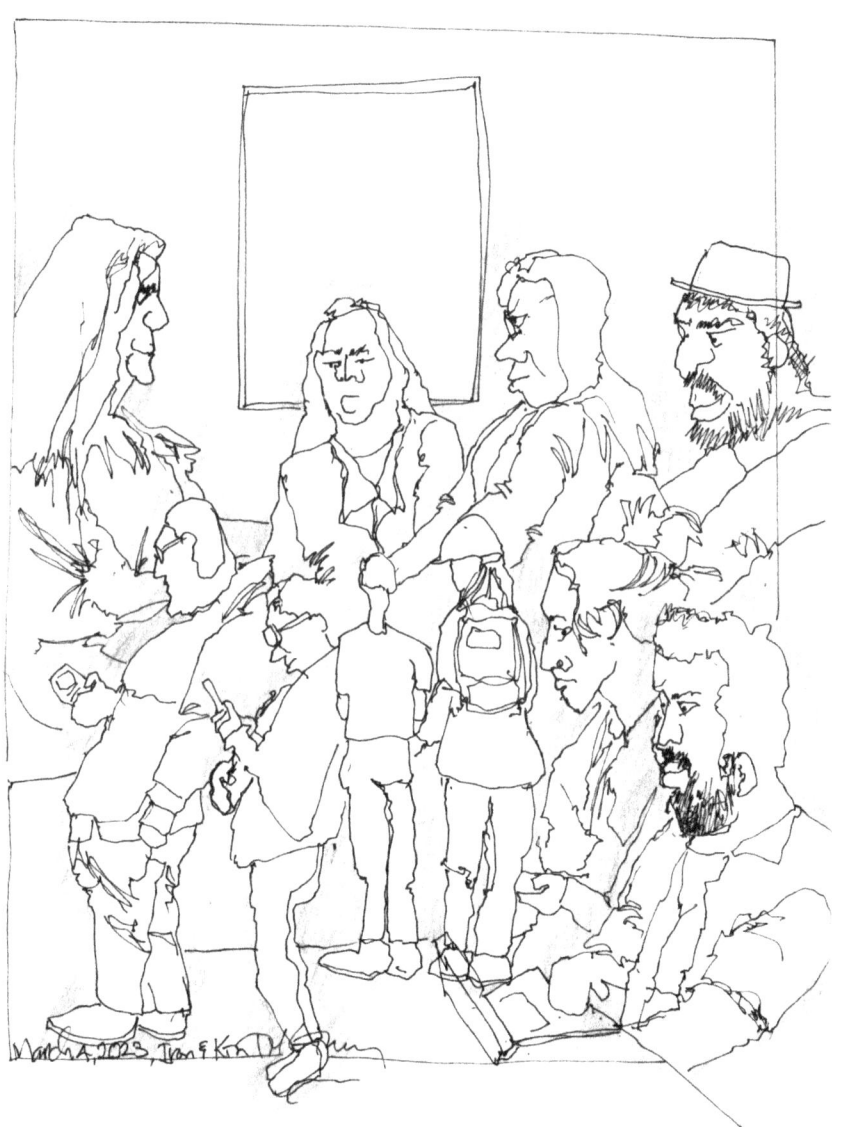

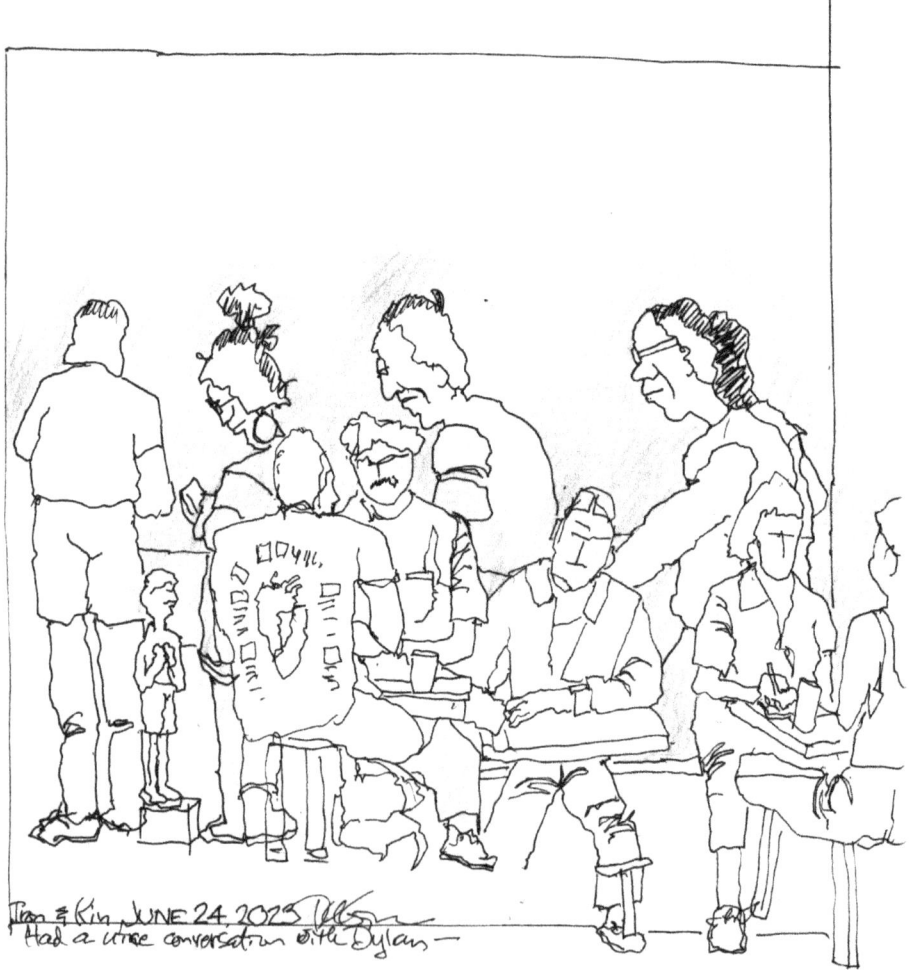

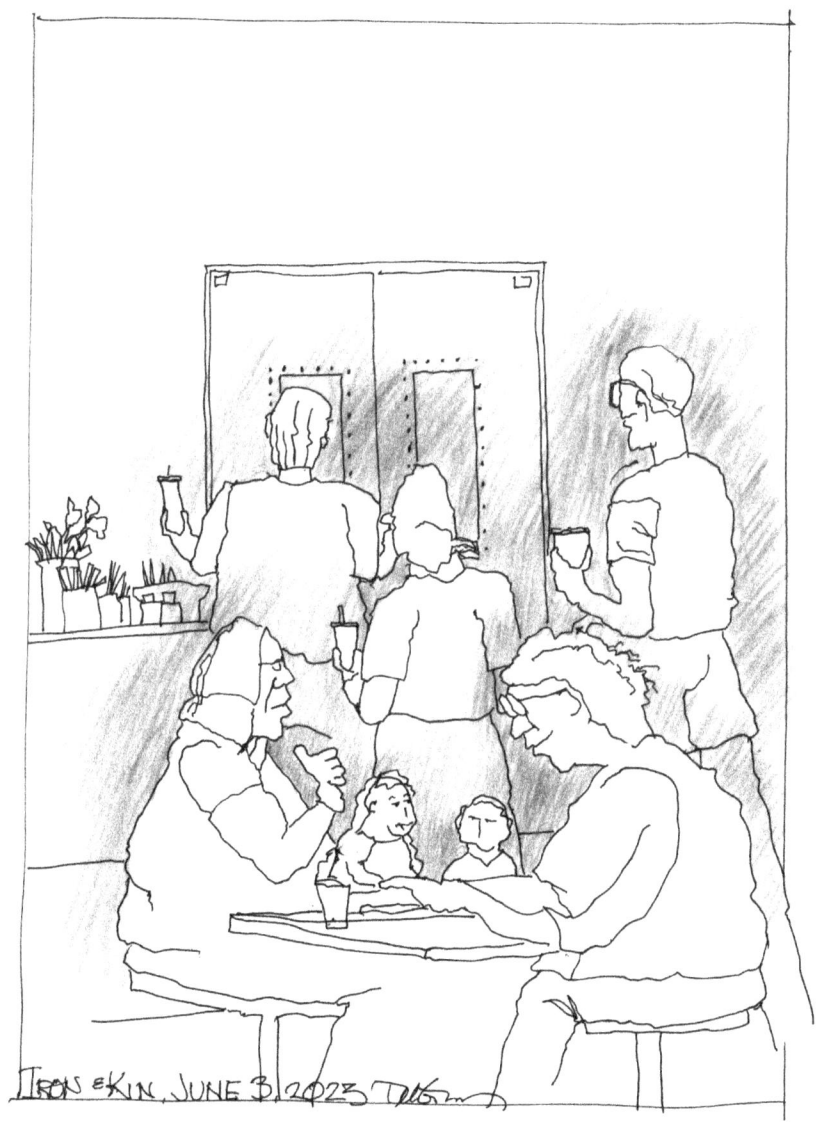

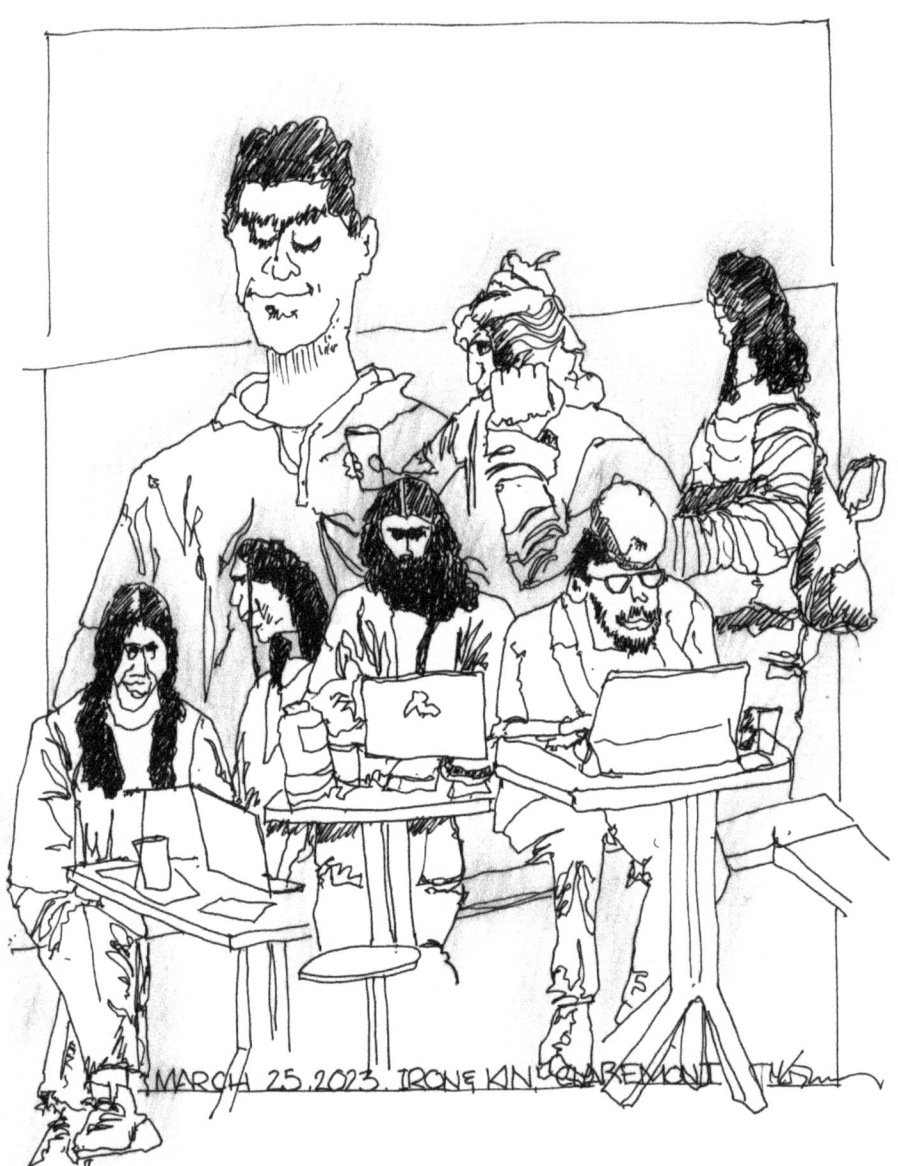

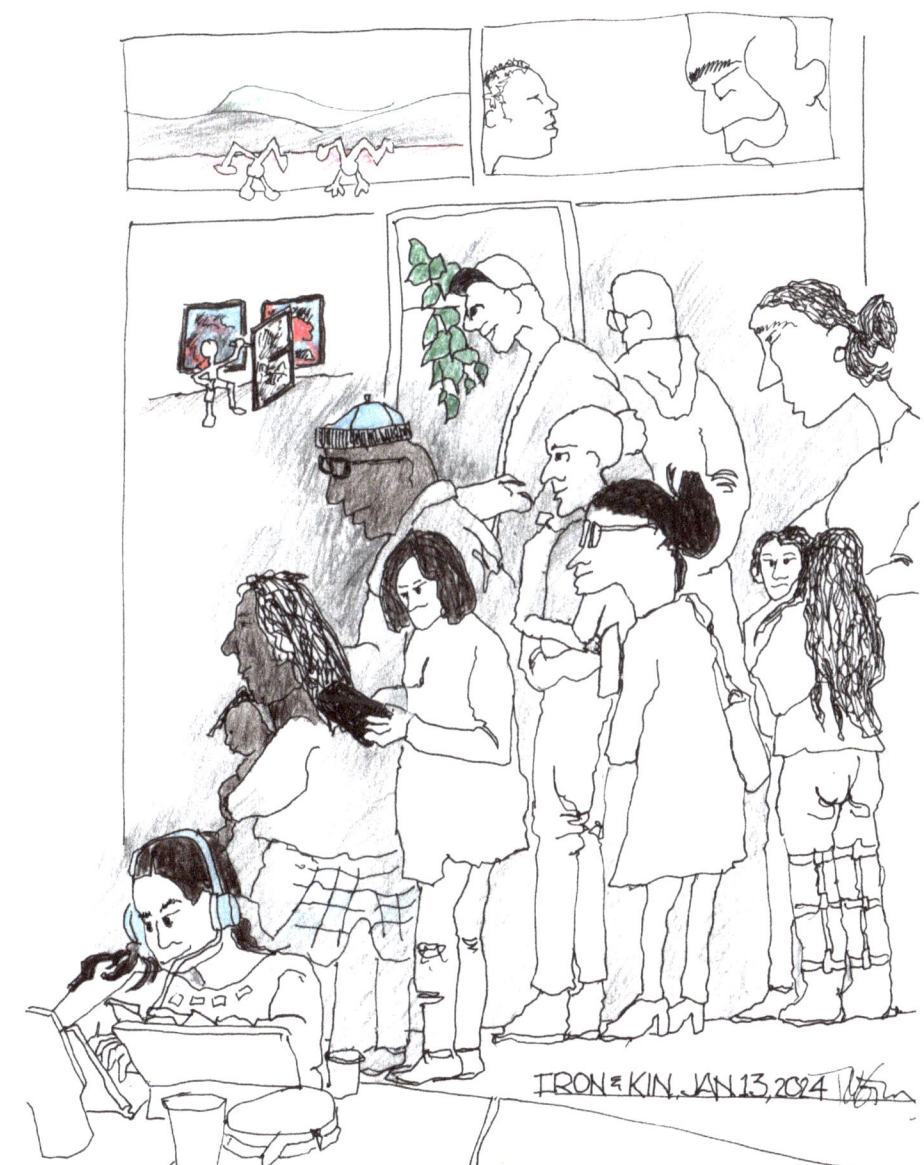

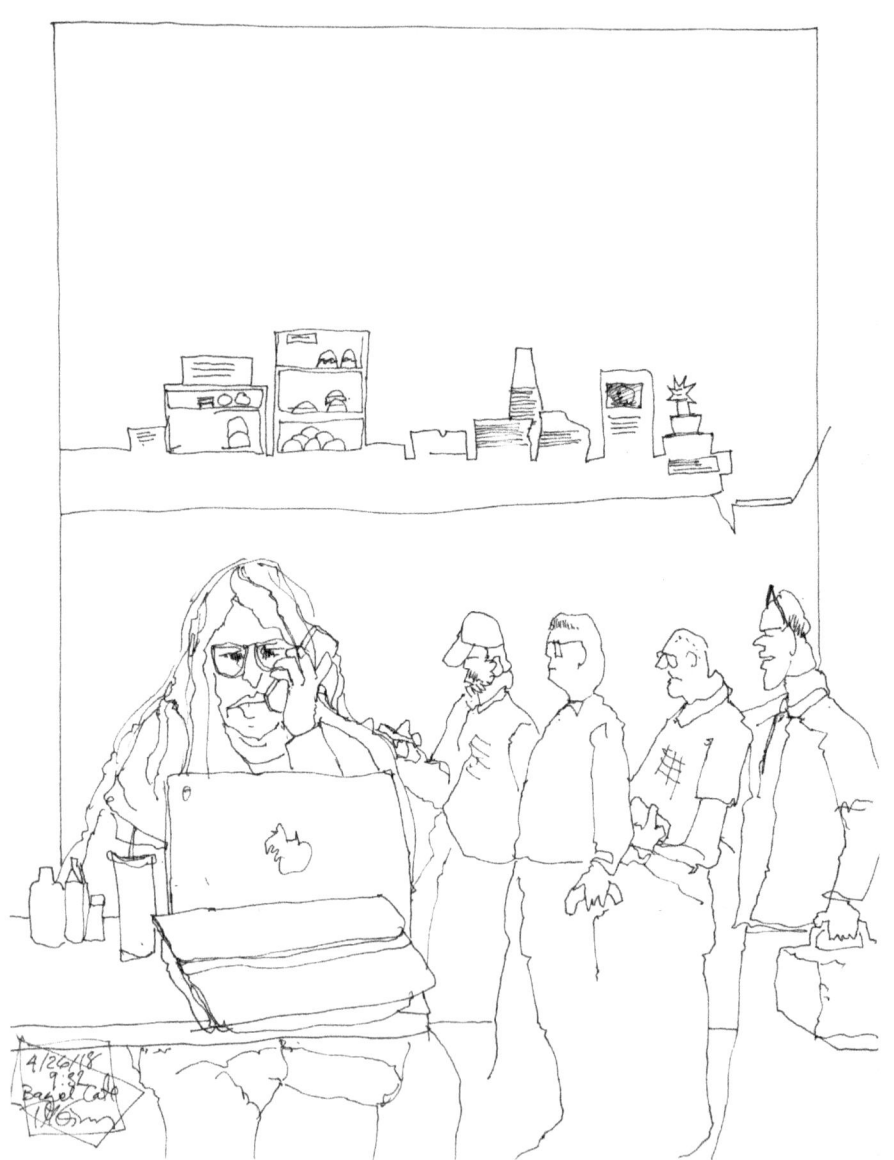

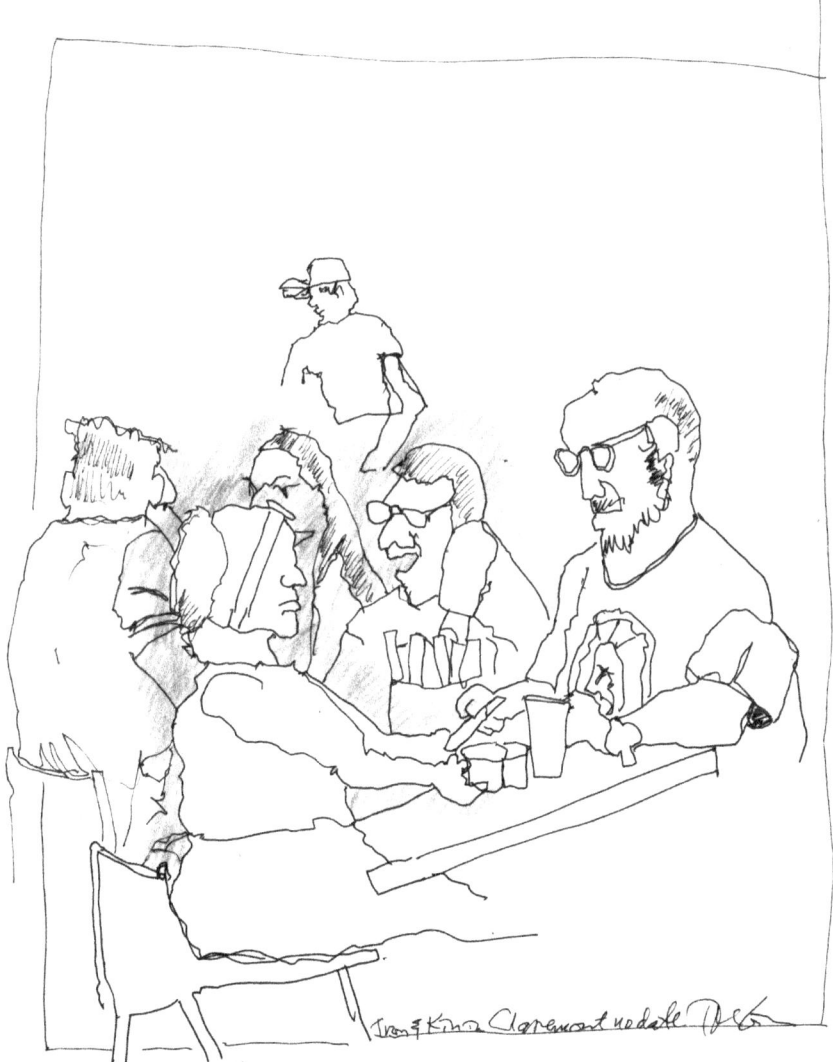

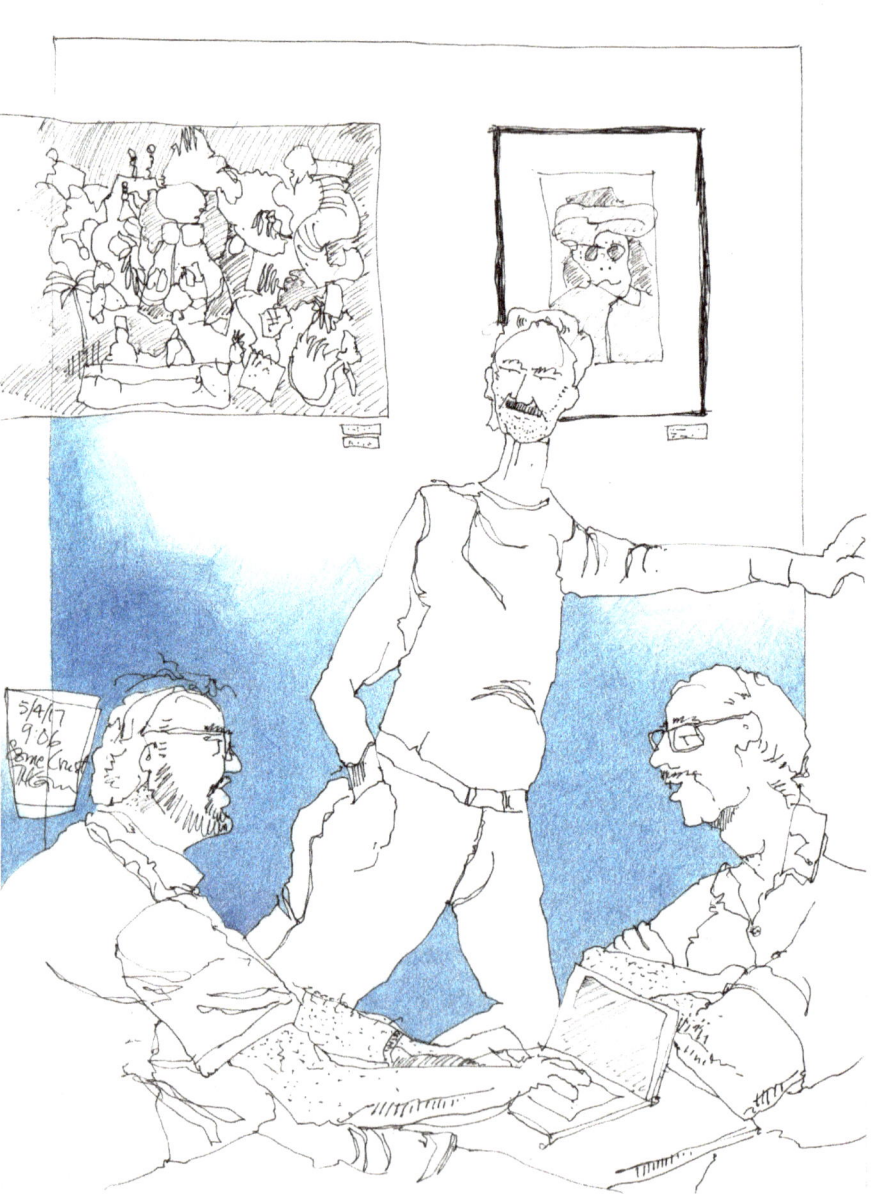

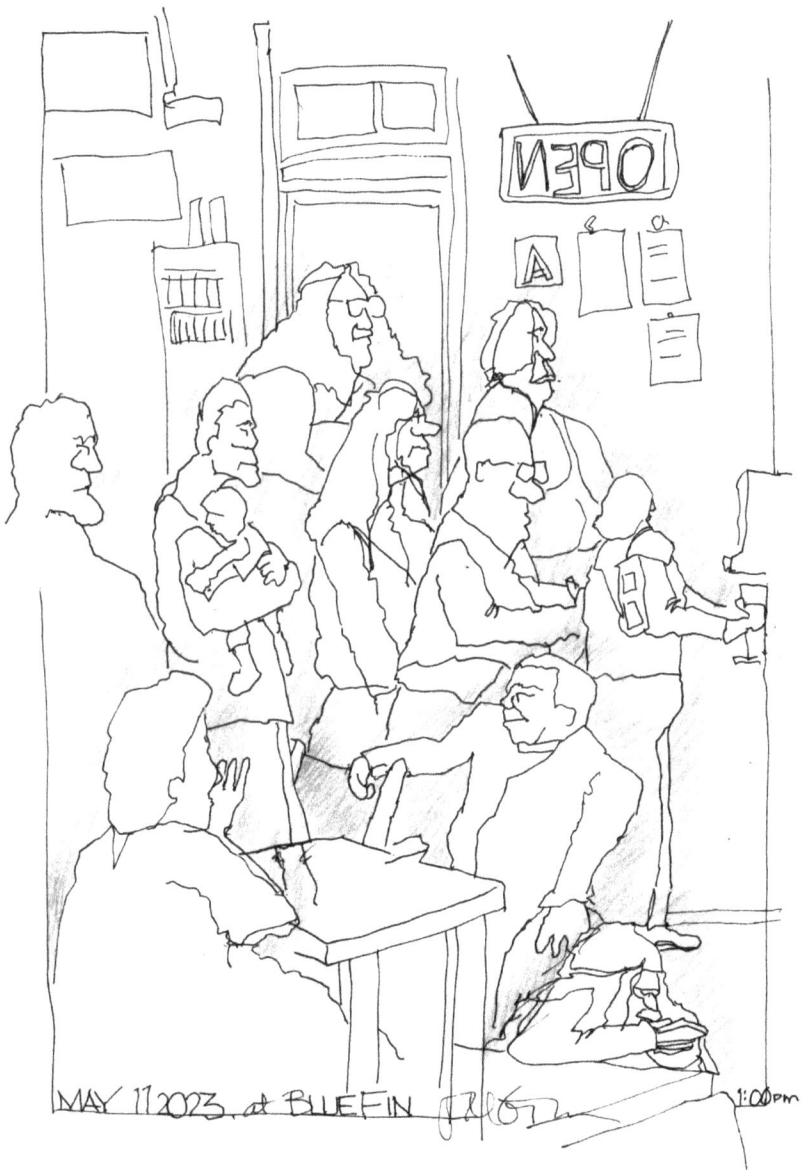

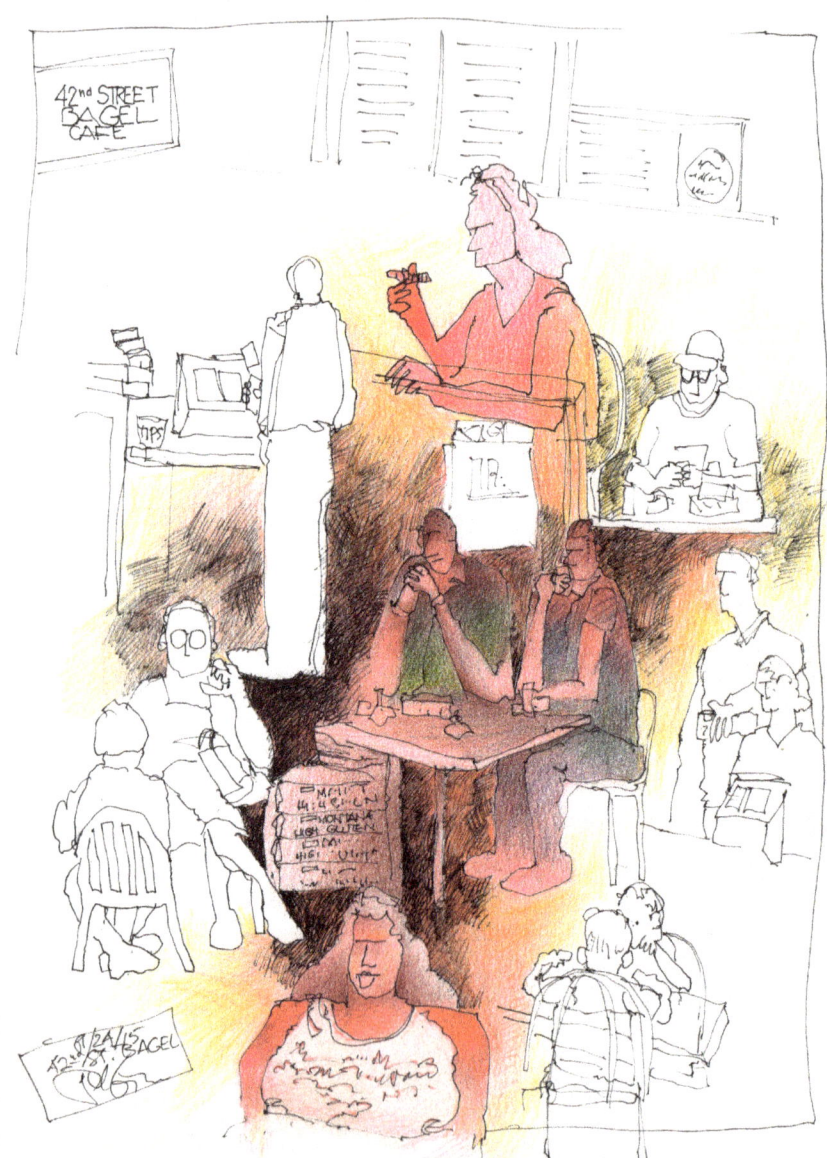

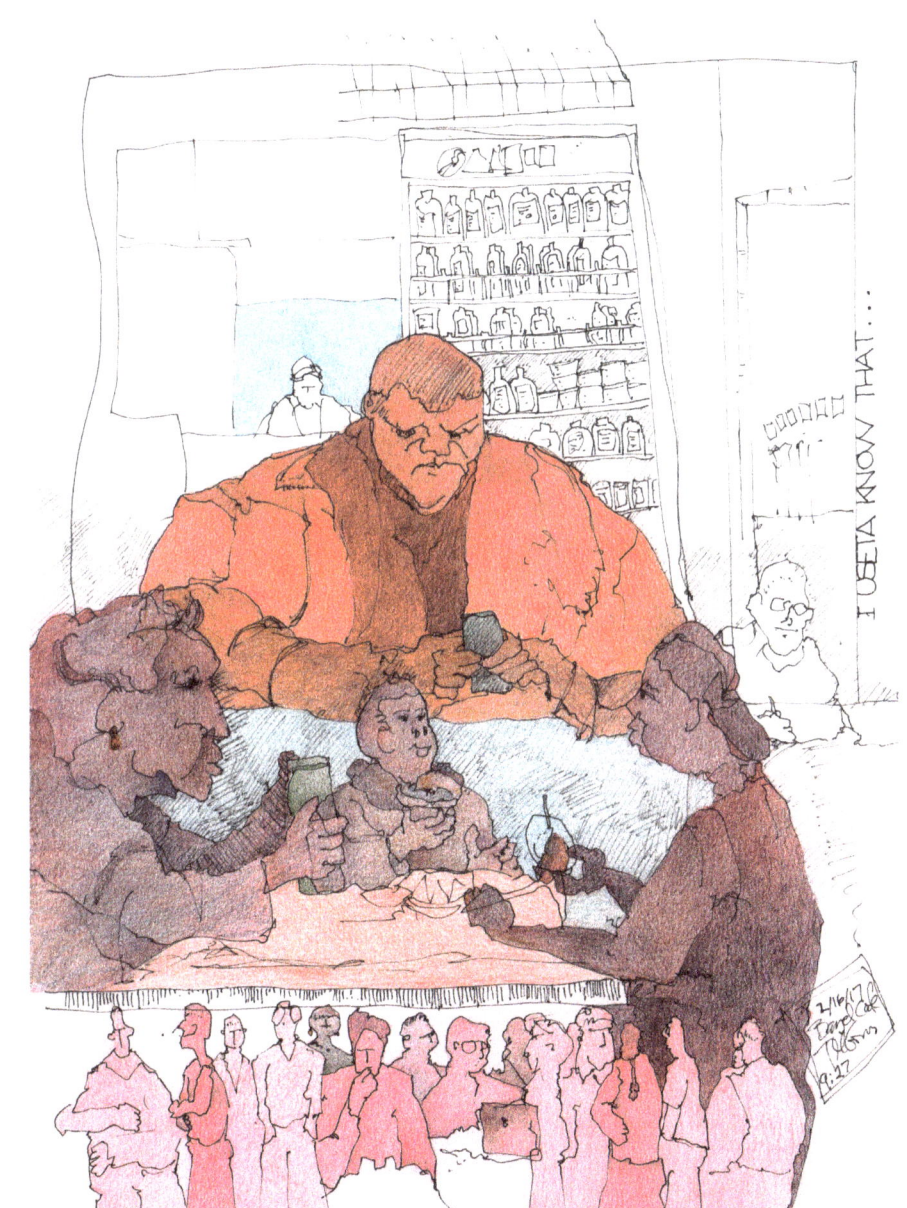

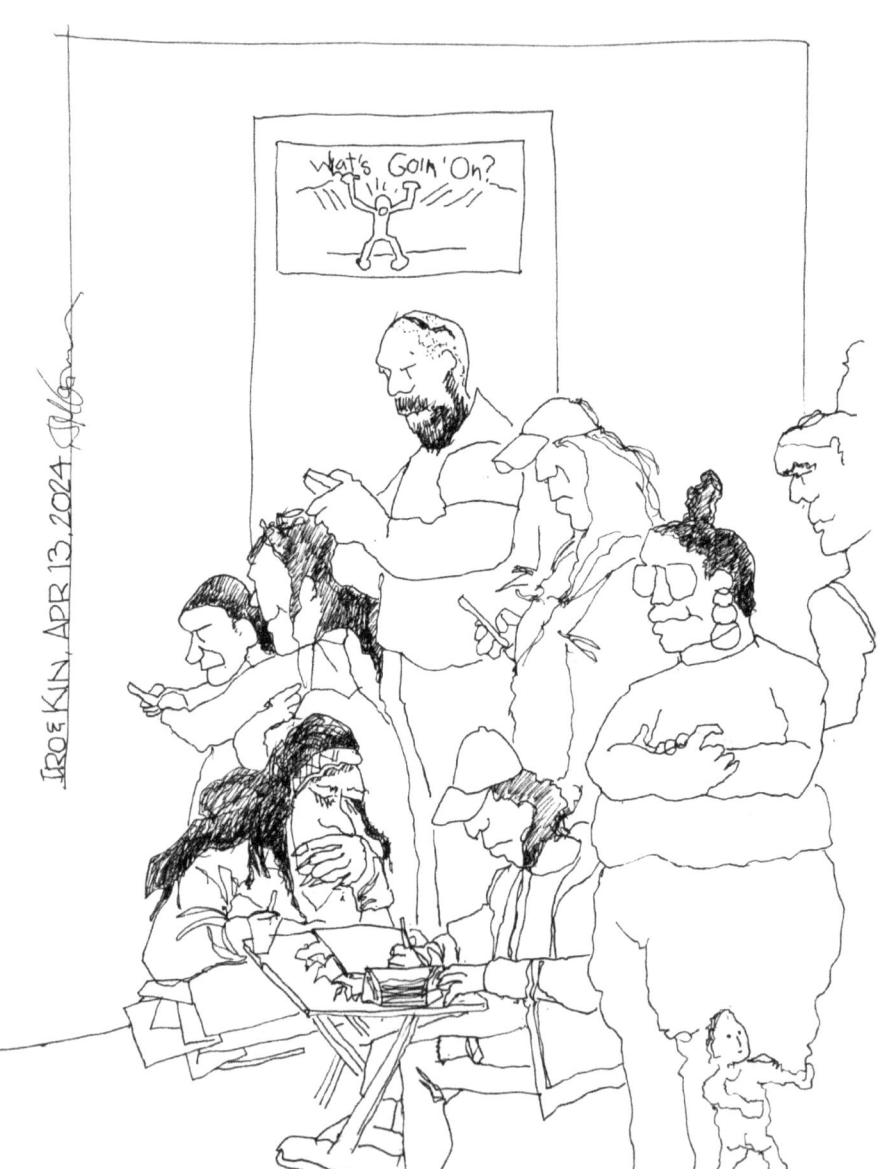

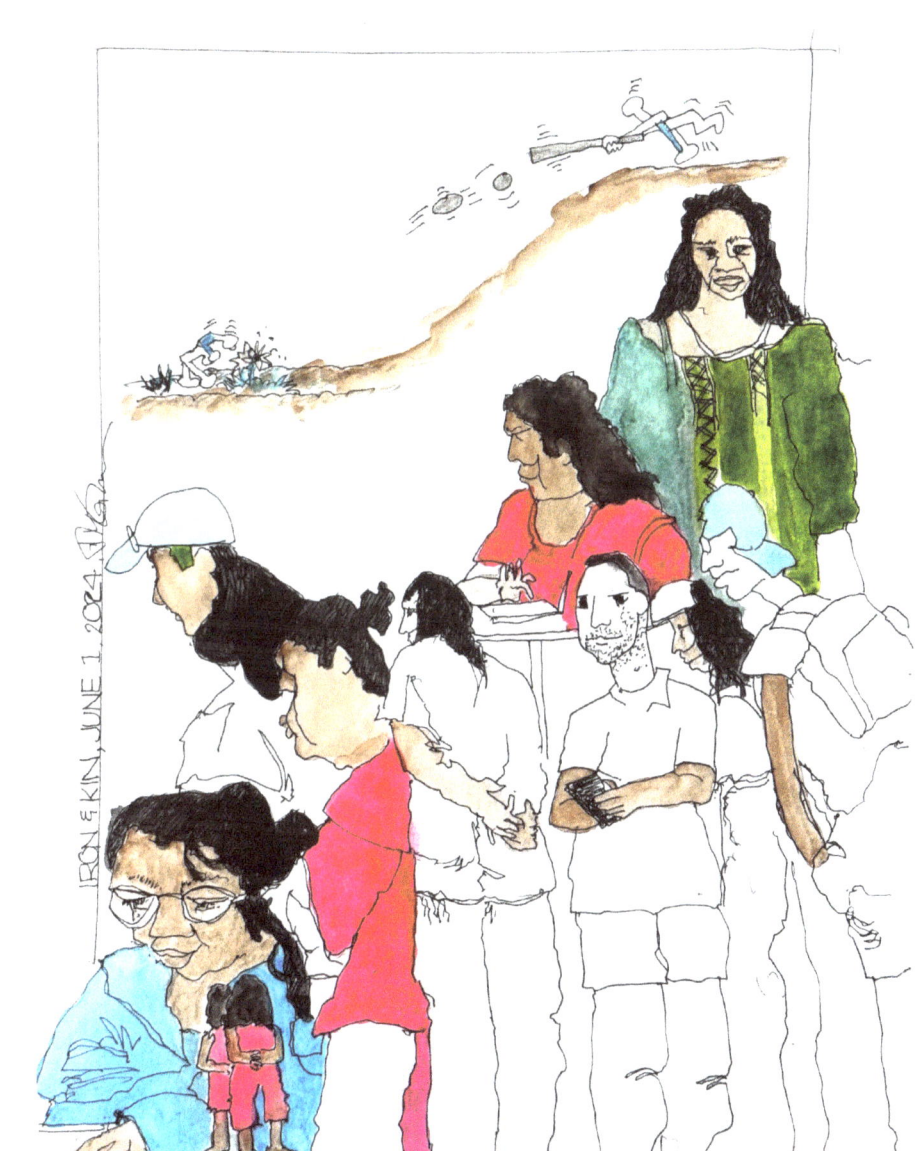

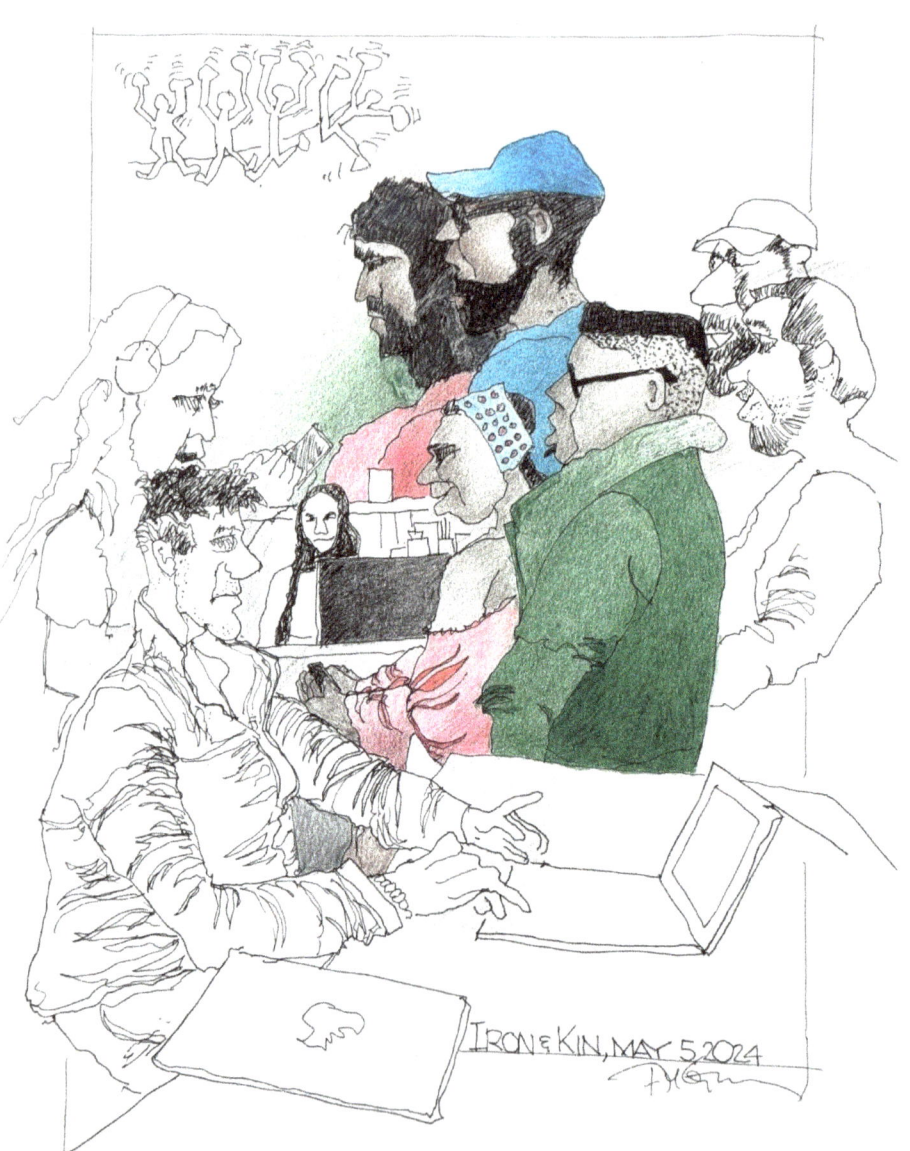

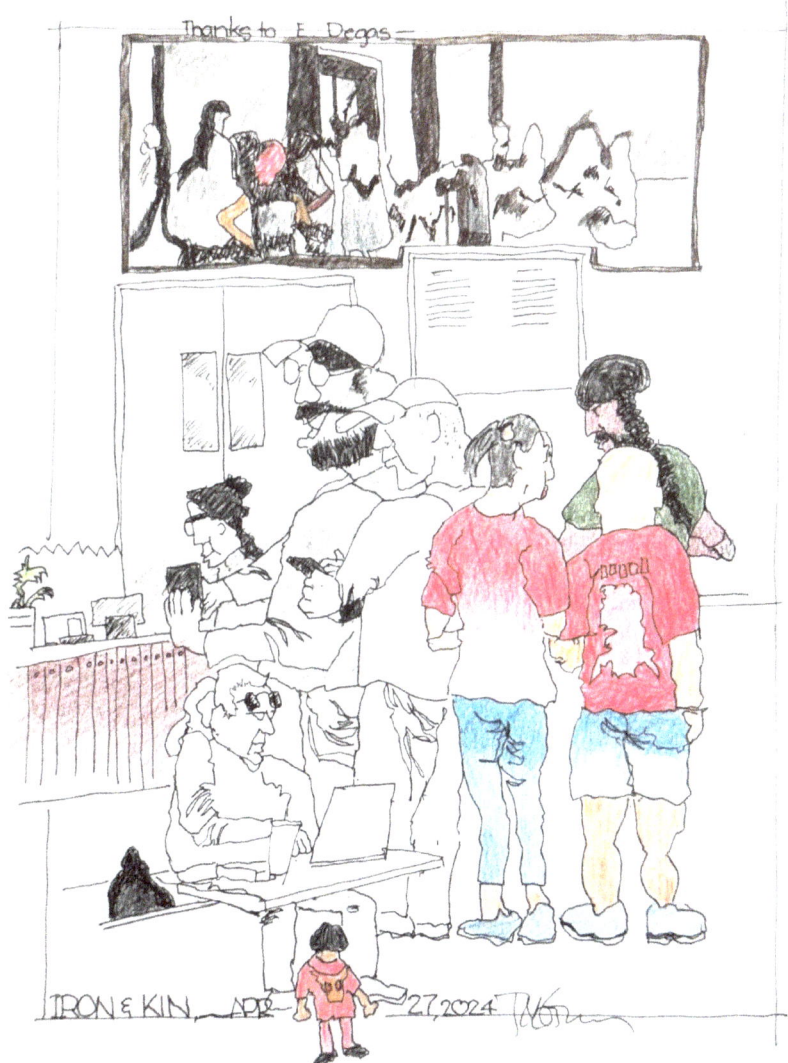

A brief conversation between TM Givens and Mark Givens

My father spent his childhood in El Monte, my mom was in Rosemead. After his stint as an Air Force photographer, he and my mom got married at the Claremont Methodist Church in 1961. They moved around a little (San Diego, La Verne, Pomona) before settling in Claremont about 1964, in Claremont Graduate School housing while my dad was at the Graduate School, then Baughman Ave, then Guilford Ave. where I spent my childhood.

He was at San Dimas High School from 1970-1989, the California Department of Education from 1991-2001, then as adjunct faculty at Cal Poly Pomona (one class here and there) from 2002-2012.

He wrote editorial cartoons for the *Pomona Clarion*, an important black newspaper published by Moody Law, prominent Claremont educator and activist. These were compiled for a book called *Diary of a Mad House-Husband* https://www.bamboodartpress.com/links/tm_givens-diary_of_a_mad_house-husband.html

This converation took place over coffee and pastries in Claremont, July 2024.

On Working

Let's start with the San Dimas High Art Department.

Well, when I first started the art department at the high school, they gave me a big room that was built for a metal shop. There were no machines in there, but it was a big room. And in the back of the room there were big counters, and on it, there were vacuums. So the kids played in those.

I had to figure out how to do an art class without any materials. They didn't have enough money to actually buy any materials.

I had a couple of kids in there that were pretty good kids. So I recruited them to go with me outside of school, and we went up and down whatever that street was. There were a lot of businesses up and down that street. Some of them were big ones, some of them were small. So we went to all of the businesses, and I told the kids that my job was to describe what we were doing, and their job was to carry whatever they were able to get.

So, that's what we did, up and down and just collected materials. And of course, most people said good luck and didn't have anything.

After two or three weeks, I realized nobody had any materials that I could fashion into something. So, we got whatever we got. At one point, there was somebody who gave us some big pieces of styrofoam that were usable. You know, the styrofoam that comes in when something big is shipped, a washing machine or whatever, you know. So that's what we used. I don't think we had any paint, it was just the big styrofoam, so that's what we did.

And the kids were kind of flustered because here they were in this big room with nothing except these big pieces of styrofoam.

So my assignment was to make something that's usable based on whatever these things looked like. And so they cut them up. They cut them up and fastened them together.

Now, we had some tape that we could put them together with. And that was the first year. That was 1971, so the cornerstone was not even there, which was established in 1971. The assignment was to make anything that was an enlargement of something that you used, or that they knew about. You can imagine what they created, big objects of cigarette packs, big things of cigarettes, or stuff that they've got at McDonald's, you know, all of those things. And we had a display in the office, in the big office where if you were registering for the school, parents and everything came in at the front. It was a big area. So that's where we put the show. I think I have some photographs of it, too.

Tossed Green Salad, wasn't that from San Dimas?

Yeah, that was the art club. Because after a few years I wanted to build an art group, but I didn't know what to call it. So I kept saying, "we're a kind of group that is made up of everything at school, kind of like a tossed green salad, you know?" Everything." So that's what it was called.

The art club also produced a magazine called *Tossed Green Salad*, which was drawings and poetry and things like that, all black and white photocopied. Was that just for the school?

Yeah, it was. And it was printed at the school. We had a guy who was a printer who did the same thing that I did, go to businesses. Except he went to specific businesses and got what they didn't want. Which was the printing presses and all of that kind of stuff, from which I have those two boxes of letterpress type. I think I gave those to you.

Yeah, I have those. I always thought those were from the packing house because, as far as I recall, there were printing presses down in the main building at the packing house. I think I might be conflating some of those events. Maybe I saw them at the packing house, and that's where I remember them.

You may have seen them there because at some point I had a studio in the old packing house, before anybody had decided to fix it all up.

That was back up in the office area, right? Was anyone else in the building?

No, I don't think so. I have some photographs of those, too.

I'd like to see those.

I don't think I took photographs of the studio but I have some photographs that I took of people running through it.

You also had a studio up at Griswold's right? You had a studio there behind the glass blower?

Yeah. Rhys Williams. He bought two or three of the pieces that I made. I brought you guys, our kids, and he made something for you. Well, maybe he didn't give them to you, but he blew them and allowed you guys to actually blow on them.

I remember that. Blowing the glass, yeah.

During that time, that's when I was making a lot of the sculptures that I made.

The wooden ones?

The little people, yeah. I thought they were really good ones. I think I have actual photos of most of the pieces that I made. I think I have prints made of those, because they were actually pretty good.

And one of them was on display at the L.A. County Museum of Art. And it was, I've forgotten which one it was, but it was open on the top and somebody tried to poke it, you know, and messed it up. I don't know how long it was out there, but it was easy to poke because it was just like the little one that I have with the poker players. It was kind of like that, and somebody poked it and knocked it down. So they took it and just put it away and didn't tell me. Until I went to pick it up.

I think that was the one I sold to a psychologist. It was two figures of me and I titled it something that was philosophical, you know, actually psychological, because it was two figures of me, and I was attacking somebody. I was attacking me on the floor, on the ground. And the psychologist said, "That was amazing! Oh, that's wonderful!" So he bought it for $500. I had to deliver it to him, but that was the only one that I really sold. The others, I'm not sure what I did.

Oh, PBS had an auction so I sent them one. And I remember the one that I sent was called "Isaac and His Son" or something. He was told by God to go and kill his son. And so I made a mountain and, you know, put the sun up on top and Isaac or whoever it was, going to get the sun with the rock. And I sent that to the PBS auction. I have no idea if it was ever sold or anything, but I assume that it was sold because I never got it back.

The high school art program eventually did get some funding.

The school gave me some money so that I could order some paint and stuff. One time we were asked to bring our art club to a painting exhibition that they were going to be involved in. Every group that was there had a car, or a van, or something, that was pulled into where we were all working. And the assignment was to paint it. We got a prize, but they did a good job painting it as if it were real because the paint was automobile paint. And they designed it and painted it right there. And it was real and we had a certain amount of time, you know, to get it done. Of course it was only on one side, they didn't paint the whole car, it was just one. And ours was a van, a white van, and that's what they did and we were awarded something, and it was fun. And I have a photograph. I took a photograph of them all standing, and it was cute. I never told them it was cute, because they're high schoolers. But it was cute because they were all in.

The foremost thing, I remember, was that my class made a bracketed banner for the basketball tournament they had every year around Christmas time. Or Thanksgiving. It was a big deal, and we always made the banner.

Now, of course, they can print those out, but then my class made them. And because I knew how to do that kind of stuff, I drew it all out on big sheets of white paper and laid it out on those big tables. And I could roll it out and they could see what I had.

And that was wonderful because we got a little bit of money from it. And the kids loved it. I did all of the lettering and all of the drawing, you know, so that all they had to do was paint it.

That's incorporating your training from General Dynamics, right? All your drafting skills.

I got that job when we were in San Diego. I couldn't find a job and I went around and talked to all of the places, you know, told them what I did and what I was going to do. It was while I was going to school. I went to school at San Diego State.

And that's where I learned about art. I took a couple of art classes.

I had a janitor job at the Methodist Student Center and we lived in a little house that was attached. So we lived in there, and that's where Karin was born.

So when I couldn't find a job, I called from San Diego, I called Don Angel who was the person that I worked for in the photo lab at General Dynamics. I had worked there while I went to Mt SAC.

We graduated from Mt SAC and then went down to San Diego and when I couldn't find a job, I called Don and he said, "Sure come on up." So that's when we moved from San Diego to Ontario and various places.

But I worked there, and the only place I could work was on third shift. The overnight shift. So that's what I did while I went to UCR.

I'd go to UCR during the day, and then when I came home, I'd have a meal or something, and then I'd go to work at General Dynamics. And that's where it was really good, because that's where I had the job of developing these big canisters that were aerial photography canisters that they would have, and they would shoot a lot of pictures from the airplane and then they'd bring the canister to me, and I put it in a big machine that I had that would develop the film from the canister. That's where I did all my work for school, all the reading and whatever. It was a big machine you just put it in there and study. I could close the door and if somebody knocked on it, I would yell, "We're working here. Just leave it outside and I'll pick it up."

And so that's what I would do, no matter what was going on. I'd yell, "Doors closed, we're working." And that's how I spent most of my time - studying and developing that. And that's how I made it through UCR.

Eventually you moved into the drafting department, right?

Yes, they closed the photo lab. Which meant, you know, goodbye photos. So I was a drafter. I did that third shift.

I think that you still employ a lot of the techniques that you developed there in the drafting department. Your lettering has a very blueprint look to it, you know? And a lot of the straight lines and all that, to me, it's got an obvious drafting feel to it.

There was a bunch of us that did this, but I did all of the big drawings that were made by engineers. They would draw something, and they were assigned what to draw and how to draw it. And then it would go to somebody who would edit the big drawing and indicate where things go - you need a plug here, or you need a wire thing here, all of that stuff. It was our job to incorporate all of the edits into the big drawing. What it was, I realized later, was a drawing of a computer chip that they had. This was a huge drawing that would make a computer chip. We didn't know what the heck people told us, and I don't know about the last part because they hid away with the photo stuff.

Before that, I was a job shopper. I worked for a company that found jobs for people. I told them I was a draftsman. And that's when I got to work with all these job shoppers in this building who were doing a lot of this stuff. Because they were doing the same kind of thing that I was doing in General Dynamics, but they were doing it for somebody else, Raytheon or something. And I worked for that group about a year. That's where I learned that there was a lot of… all those guys who were working there were "free." When they got paid, they got paid in cash. They could go to a bank and cash their check, or whatever money they had, and they never had a bank. They didn't go to doctors. They got all their health care from schools, the dentistry school. All of that. So I questioned them about that, and they said, "yeah, we don't have any attachment to anything. I mean, we don't. That's it. This is the only thing we do." "I'll be damned," I thought. Yeah, they do. They have it. They got paid, and it was pretty good pay, too. But they got paid, and they didn't owe anything to anybody or whatever. They just saved what they had.

And was that appealing to you?

Yeah. Not to your mom. But, yes, it was appealing to me. I thought, this is the way to live. But we moved to Pomona, and I got a job at General Dynamics. That was more my job.

After San Dimas High School, you moved to Sacramento and went into the advocacy side of things, right? I mean, you got out of the classroom and more into the administrative side.

Delaine Eastin, I think she's gone now, but she was the California superintendent of public instruction, and she was the superintendent that I was under. I worked there for 10 years and for half that time, I worked in the arts in education office up there on the fifth floor. I applied for it and didn't realize that what I was doing was applying for a job with the state. What I was doing was down with the arts and history office. That was fun. A friend of mine and I, Ron, worked with Huell Howser, and we did the Teacher's Book for some of his shows. Sometimes he came up with his crew and went to all of the little places. But we knew him.

I remember the one where it was about pigeons that flew from Santa Monica to Catalina. Because they didn't have any intercoms, there was nothing like that that they could communicate back and forth, so they had pigeons that they would tie some kind of a message and send them. And they would fly over to Catalina to wherever they were supposed to fly. So that, and that was one of the ones that we wrote down all of what the teacher was supposed to do and how they were. And anyway, that was fun.

On Drawing

When you're drawing people do you make up some sort of backstory? How do you how approach these drawings - the standing in line the coffee shop drawings?

That's interesting. That's one of the things I think about. When I look at different people standing in line, I think I truly want to get a reference. So, I start with the forehead and usually draw the face. But I think mainly what I do—I don't think about where they are, or what they're doing, or anything like that—I only think about them when I see that they're doing something unusual. I always try to draw the hands. Almost everybody's looking into computer, which is interesting. I don't know what they're talking about but sometimes they laugh, HA HA HA, you know, as if this computer is a real person. Maybe it is, you know? I don't know but I always try and get them when they're laughing.

Of course, that's not always easy to do because they're moving. And I usually try and get them when their backs are to me because then I can draw a little bit of their face, but then they turn away. "Damn," you know, "why can't they stay still? Don't they know I'm drawing?"

There's one I have now where the guy's hair was orange. I mean bright orange! In the same line there were two people - her arm was always around him. She was blonde, a beautiful blonde, and he was black and I thought, "If Trump was president that wouldn't happen." So I drew him like that, just thinking. So the guy with the orange hair and the couple... that was interesting.

So you're documenting, observing, the time we live in, the people around us, and the culture that is there.

I hadn't really thought about the culture, but that's true. I had this idea when I was taking photographs of people as I walked down Indian Hill, if I take notice of something, wherever I look, it must have been interesting to me to look at it, so I take a photograph. So I take the same idea that I had—that if I look at somebody I must have noticed them because I wouldn't have looked at them if I hadn't noticed them—so I try and draw that. Because I think that's kind of the way I work. If I noticed something, I don't know why I looked at it but I must have looked at it for a reason.

Speaking of photography, you did that in the air force, right?

When I was doing photography for the air force, there was a big earthquake in one of the small towns not too far from Casablanca, where I was—I forgot the name of the city—but it wiped out the city and they sent me down to take photographs. I took a lot of photographs, some of which I think I still have, but it was of people doing stuff. All I had to do was notice that they were doing something and then I took that photograph. I didn't even have to find out anything about it, other than that they were Americans doing something, helping people in a foreign land. I mean, it was upsetting, but that was the purpose of that.

The similarities that I see in *that* work and in these drawings, is that you are capturing the environment around you, and because you have a photographer's eye and an illustrator's eye, you frame shots, you frame the scene. Even when the people in the coffee shop are not in the right places, or they move or whatever, you can put them where you want them to be and you can frame a shot the way that you want it to look. So it's not a snapshot, as you've said before, it's not a portrait, it's a picture. So what you're doing is setting up this picture to document this moment.

>Purposefully, yeah. Sometimes I'll see somebody in the line that's noticeable—either they're really tall, or big and fat, or something like that, you know? Somebody that I should draw. Or often there's somebody there who looks like they're just standing there looking and won't move, and so I'll draw them and that's exactly what they look like. They look like they're just a person that just *does* that—stand very still and doesn't move—and the whole line moves but that person stays right there. And I think, "Wow, yeah, that's an odd person."
>
>I don't think that until I look at the drawing later and say, "Oh my god, yeah, that guy stayed there *the whole time. What was he doing?*" He could have been thinking, he could have been just looking, you know? But I never *know* that, I just know that that's what he's done.

The drawings that were displayed in 2018 at the Botanic Garden in Claremont, the "100 Garden Views" exhibit, were made while sitting at each one of the memorial benches in the Garden, drawing what you see from each bench. And then the *Garden Prayers* books (on Pelekinesis) collected those drawings and arranged them by season.

> The reason I was sitting there was thinking about why the person who wanted to donate that bench, which was expensive to do, why did they pick that particular spot? Well, I assume that it was because they were looking at something that person would have would have liked. So I just sat there and I thought about that.

So by sitting on the bench and thinking about what that person would be observing and then what is being observed is a conversation between the person sitting on the bench and the thing they're looking at.

> Right. Well, that's interesting. It doesn't make any sense because when I'm drawing that tree, or whatever, I'm not thinking of that. I'm only thinking of that when I get home and try to put some color on it. That's when I think about *how did it happen* and *what made it happen? How it's beautiful* and *it's really structurally odd. How did it do that all by itself?* Well, it may not have done it all by itself.

So the time for contemplation, it seems, is when you get home and look at what you've done, and add color or that kind of thing. Like you were saying about the orange hair - that was what captured your attention and then, when you get home and apply the color to the black and white, that's when you start thinking about the color of the hair and the people. Do you create back stories for the characters or do you just think about the character that's on the page?

I don't know. That's a hard thing to ask because I have a hard time thinking about what I'm thinking. That's meta-cognition. Haha. Don't get me started!

I think I told you a story about when I was doing a drawing at the church and the man sitting next to me said, "Do you *see* that line that you're drawing when you draw it?" I thought, "Huh. That's a stupid question." How could I answer that? I couldn't answer it.

But I think it was you that said, "Well, maybe that was the critical question." What do I see before I draw? I don't know, but that's what I ask when I start drawing because that's what I do. And I look at those little drawings that I've done and ask, "why did I do that? Did I do that on purpose?" I must have done something; I must have looked at that and said, "Well this is how I observe that," but I don't think I thought about that. I just did it.

Some of the small characters, the little cartoon characters that you put in there, are doing things. Recently you did the one where it's a drawing of people in a coffee shop and then there's a small inset piece of a car in a field. What was that about?

Well that was part of the story that I tell about me and my dad going out looking for my first car. We found it with that guy and he sold me that car—my '49 Ford—for a hundred dollars. That's what I had and that's what we bought. I don't know how it relates to the other drawing, or if it does, but that's what I thought about when I was wondering what I should draw. I don't know if the big drawing from Iron and Kin relates to that but maybe it does. I have no idea.

Those small inset pieces are kind of what you're thinking about as you're doing this big drawing. Sometimes these little characters are just angry, or throwing a tantrum, or cheering, or something. But sometimes it'll be a reflection on, for example, your master's thesis show and so you'll have these little drawings of the paintings that you did for that show and then these characters are manipulating these little paintings. There's also a great one of two little creatures who stumble upon a car and then the car gets beamed away on a spaceship. It's really funny, just little comics there.

Well, I think there's three of those like that. When I drew that originally—it was many years before I made this one—it was a big drawing that was done serially. I had all of the individual scenes of that particular car kind of driving along and then stopping somewhere and then something happens because I think it was in trees or something and then continued going on and then stopping and getting something, you know, on and on and that's kind of what I thought about at that point, that it was just a big cartoon that I had thought about a long time ago. That was fun to draw.

You have collected some wonderful original comic art from people like Jim Berry, Charles Schultz, Milton Caniff, and the *Prince Valiant*, of course. With this comic art, I can see the influences in your drawings. The way that these drawings are framed reminds me a great deal of single panel editorial cartoons you did for the *Clarion*. Do you think that one has influenced the other, or is that just the way you see?

Yes, I do and I never really even thought about that, but I am so conscious about making sure that every drawing I do has a frame on it and that's from all the cartoons that I have. I still put something down at the bottom that says what this drawing is, a date and a place. And if I was to draw a cartoon, this is the way I'd do it. But I'm not smart enough to draw cartoons because I don't think about cartoons the way I see cartoons. I see those as brilliant things that run across the page, have a beginning and an ending and in between, and I can't think about that. You know, I can think about *this* and *this*.

When I was drawing cartoons for the *Clarion*, that's what I could think about. I remember the one that I made when Angela Davis was released from jail, that's what I drew, you know. When she was released from jail, that was a good thing.

Now, I don't know how many I recently have done that the little guys echo what I'm drawing, I don't know about that, but somebody could probably interpret what those are.

A lot of what you're talking about is the process, right? You've talked about "process theology" before, which is related, and I've been thinking about the process of making music, of creation, and how that, in and of itself, is an important thing for a person to do. What you're doing is like process art, you know? It's not about the end result necessarily, but sometimes it's about the creation, it's about the process of sitting and doing the drawing.

Well I think it's more Buddhist than Christian, but I think I have to read more about Buddhist stuff than I do about religion because I can understand that. I don't think I can relate it to something, but I think that's more about what I believe.

I would rather think about a spiritual being that is not called that spiritual being by a name but that's what I'm believing. And I see the reflection of the yellow flowers and I kind of like that. I like the way they're moving and I can relate those movements to a spiritual being. I'm not sure I can understand why. Reading all about it until I saw both the real wind blowing that color around, I think that's pretty because I like the movement, but that's it. That's interesting.

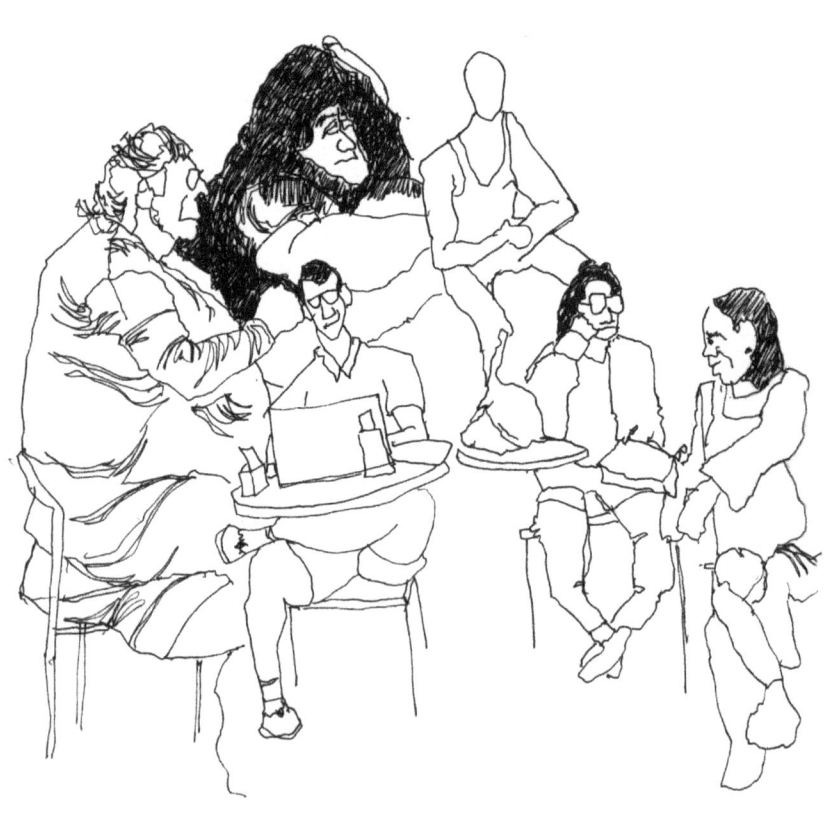

About the Author

Terry Givens and his wife Carolyne were married in Claremont, California in 1961.

He finished his education in Art History and Painting at UCR and the Claremont Graduate School and has participated in many Claremont events, namely exhibits at the Claremont Community Foundation and as a featured artist at the Taste of Claremont, sponsored by the Rotary Club of Claremont.

Terry has exhibited in a variety of media, with sculpture at the Ankrum Gallery, the Los Angeles County Museum of Art, Chaffey College, and with drawings and paintings in a variety of galleries in Sacramento. In 2018, the Rancho Santa Ana Botanic Garden exhibited his drawings in a changing exhibition titled "Terry Givens: 100 Garden Views." He has contributed many drawings to organizations, individuals, and businesses in and around Claremont.

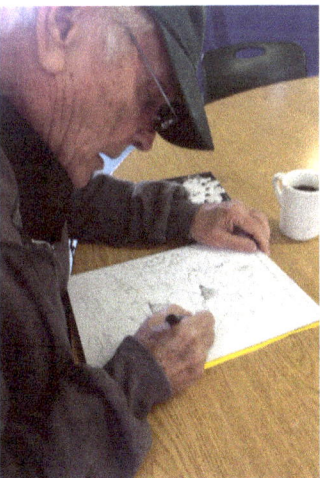

PHOTO BY CAROLYNE GIVENS

In addition, he has curated exhibitions at the Rex Wignall Gallery in Ontario and the Riverside Art Museum.

He taught art and photography in a variety of local elementary and secondary schools, as well as at local universities and colleges.

The series *Garden Prayers*, inspired by his Botanic Garden exhibit, and a book of photographs from the 1968 March on Washington were both published by Pelekinesis.

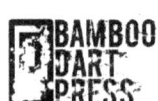

112 N. Harvard Ave. #65

Claremont, CA 91711

chapbooks@bamboodartpress.com

www.bamboodartpress.com

www.ingramcontent.com/pod-product-compliance
Lightning Source LLC
Chambersburg PA
CBHW040547220526
45473CB00017B/3048